FIRST DRAFT

The Publishers wish to thank the
European Community Commission
whose generous support made the
translation and publication of this
book possible.

NIKA TURBINA

FIRST DRAFT

Poems

Introduction by

Yevgeny Yevtushenko

Translations by

Antonina W. Bouis
and Elaine Feinstein

MARION BOYARS
London · New York

Published in Great Britain and the United States in 1988
Reprinted in 1988
by Marion Boyars Publishers
24 Lacy Road, London SW15 1NL
26 East 33rd Street, New York, NY 10016

Distributed in the United States by
Kampmann & Co, New York

Distributed in Canada by
Book Center Inc, Montreal

Distributed in Australia by
Wild & Woolley Pty, Glebe, N.S.W.

First published in Moscow, USSR, 1984

British Library Cataloguing in Publication Data

Turbina, Nika
   First draft.
   I. Title
   891.71'44   PG3489.U6/

Library of Congress Cataloging in Publication Data

Turbina, Nika, 1974—
   First draft.
   Translated from the Russian.
   1. Turbina, Nika, 1974—   —Translations, English.
I. Bouis, Antonina W.   II. Feinstein, Elaine.   III. Title.
PG3489.U63A23   1987   891.71'44   87-22403

ISBN 0-7145-2864-1

Typeset by Ann Buchan (Typesetters), Surrey
and printed in Great Britain by
St Edmundsbury Press Ltd, Bury St Edmunds, Suffolk

CONTENTS

AN EIGHT YEAR-OLD POET

The eight year-old poet's name is Nika Turbina. She was born on December 17, 1974 in Yalta and, by an amazing coincidence, is at the very school in Yalta where once upon a time Marina Tsvetayeva attended high school. Nika's grandfather — Anatoli Ignatievich Nikanorin — is a poet, the author of several volumes of poetry. But lots of people study in Tsvetayeva's school and lots of people have poets for grandfathers.

It is no accident that I call Nika a poet and not a poetess. From my point of view an eight year-old poet is a rarity and perhaps even a miracle. A child once wrote the lines: 'Let there always be the sun, let there always be mama, let there always be me,' which became the refrain of a famous song. But those were only lines that expressed a child's talent, not a poet's talent. There are authors of lines and there are poets. A poet is one whose lines form a unity — the author's character, his image. From our adult point of view, a child isn't even a poem but only its opening line. Can something that is only forming form an image? Rarely, but it can. Most examples come from music: let us recall, first and foremost, Mozart. The Italian conductor Willi Ferrero became world famous before he was ten but neither he nor our violinist Busya Goldshtein, who gave major concerts at an early age, became geniuses as expected. But they did remain solid professionals, which is also no small thing.

Did they not as children give adult listeners the rare joy of a miracle? Roberto Loretti's voice lost its divine charm with age, but even to this day his thin voice singing 'Santa Lucia' resounds in our grateful memories.

When you come across a rare early talent in children, you should not worry ahead of time that they might be spoiled by excessive attention. It is more dangerous not to give that attention in time. If it is necessary for adults, then why not give it to children? It must be admitted that in the case of artist Nadya Rusheva the acclaim was belated in her lifetime. Not out of hostility but bewilderment in the face of her 'non-childlike' drawings. We have created incredible conditions in our country for the development of art and culture in children. But sometimes we 'overorganize' this development, approach it with preconceived adult paradigms, beginning in nursery schools and kindergartens to saddle children with rather coarse sloganlike verses, written in pseudochild's language. The magazine *Komsomolskaya Pravda* has written justly about this more than once. For some reason we try to develop a childish culture in children and are frightened by any manifestation of adulthood. But maturity in children is a phenomenon requiring the most caring and tactful noninterference combined with the most caring and tactful support.

Nika Turbina was discovered by *Komsomolskaya Pravda*, which printed her major cycle when she was eight, and then central television invited her to read her poetry to an audience of millions when she was not yet nine. I must admit that I missed the publication and did not see her on the screen, but from every side I heard the most varied reactions, some awed, some cautious — 'I hope they don't drive the child crazy, turning her into a wunderkind' — and some out-and-out suspicious — 'She couldn't have written them herself. . . . They're much too adult.'

As a high school student, Tsvetayeva wrote:

> For my verses, as for precious wines
> the time will come. . .

But, Tsvetayeva was fifteen then, and here we have an eight year-old. In the context of today's catastrophic increase in the median age of young poets, now reaching forty, it seems almost improbable that Mayakovsky had written *A Cloud in Trousers* when he was 'handsome and twenty-two.' And now we have an eight year-old poet. . . An unexpected leap, covering the gaping emptiness of several generations. Perhaps because we are so eager for new, bright names, impatience might fool us in our appreciation?

I was sceptical until the summer of 1983 when I met Nika at Pasternak's house in Peredelkino. I went there with my English translator Arthur Boyars and my publisher Marion Boyars after a visit to Pasternak's grave. I asked them if they would like to see Pasternak's house which was kept exactly as it had been in Pasternak's life time by his daughter-in-law. By chance Nika Turbina and her mother were visiting from Yalta. Over a cup of tea I asked Nika to recite her poems to us. After the first few lines I lost all my doubts — her poems were not the fruit of literary mystification. Only poets can read like that. In her voice I could sense a special, I would say a sustained, ringing. Later, at my request, Nika's mother gave me everything she had written and I realized that what I had before me was more than individual poems — I had a book, because everything came together into the image of a personality.

I found quite a few weaknesses in her poems but I did not want to impose my corrections on Nika — I wanted her to make them herself. Nika defended her poems with the dignity of a small queen who felt the weight of a heavy metal crown on her head. Thus, for instance, I could not convince her that the word for nettles (*krapíva*) was not stressed on the last syllable. I suggested that she replace it with *tryn-travá*. Nika resisted. 'I've heard peasants say *krapivá*.' Nika knows her own worth. But never once did I feel that this was the conceit of a spoiled child: it was only the natural difficulty of thought about her difficult craft. When Nika agreed to something, it came with difficulty, as it should have morally. Only after inner re-evaluation. She does not yet have professional tricks but she does have a professional respect for the writer's craft. This book was edited only with her participation.

Nika Turbina's book is a unique phenomenon not only because

it is written by an eight year-old girl. This book makes one think that children in general perceive the world in a much more adult way than we think. But not all children know how to express that and Nika does. There is much that is purely private, diary-like, in this book. But still, one should pause and think over its many tragic intonations, for other children must have the same acute sense of contemporaneity, the burning sense of someone's lies, and of tackiness, and the aching sense of anxiety for our planet.

Nika's poetic diary, thanks to its vulnerable sincerity, becomes the diary of other children, those who do not write poetry.

Will Nika ever become a professional poet? Who knows . . .

She herself answered the question seriously and cautiously:

'I don't know. My fate will tell . . . But it seems to me that that is not the important thing.'

'What is the important thing for you?'

Nika thought. 'The important thing is truth . . . I began composing verse out loud when I was three . . . I banged my fists on the piano and composed . . . The poems came to me as something incredible that comes to you and then leaves . . . But for now it hasn't left. Like a dream that doesn't leave. When I write, I have the feeling that a person can do anything if he only wants to . . . There are so many words inside that you get lost. A person must understand that his life is not long. And if he values his life, then his life will be long, and if he deserves it, it will be eternal, even after death.'

Nika's answer to the question of who was her favourite poet, I admit, amazed me.

'Mayakovsky.'

I burst out, 'But you're nothing like him . . .'

Nika replied, 'That doesn't matter. His poetry gives me strength. I can go farther and farther . . .'

Nika and I chose the title for this volume from one of her poems. An eight year-old child is in some sense a first draft of a person. As forms of poetic thought are born and expanded in a draft, the features of future moral maturity develop in a child.

I hope that as readers pick up this slim book and open it they will enter the complex secret world not simply of an eight year-old child but of an eight year-old poet and will think once more of the many spiritual riches with which our children are endowed and of the fact that we must guard these riches from the threat of destruction that hangs over the heads of the children of the world.

Yevgeny Yevtushenko

A NOTE ON THE TRANSLATORS

All of the seventy-six poems in this volume were initially translated into literal versions by Antonina W. Bouis. Thirty-three of these (marked 'E.F.' in the text) were rendered into poetic form by Elaine Feinstein. The rest (marked 'A.B.' in the text) were recast by Antonina W. Bouis.

Antonina W. Bouis has published over twenty books in translation from the Russian. Authors include Andrei Voznesensky, Yevgeny Yevtushenko, Dimitri Shostakovich (memoirs), Vassily Aksyonov, Vladimir Orlov and the Strugatsky brothers. Her work has been highly acclaimed in the United States and in England. She lives in New York.

Elaine Feinstein is a renowned English poet and novelist. She has published five volumes of poetry of which *Badlands* is the latest, has written eight novels, including the brilliant *Borders*, and has translated four Soviet poets: Bella Akhmadulina, Yunna Morits, Margerita Aliger and Marina Tsvetayeva, whose biography *A Captive Lion* she published in 1986. Elaine Feinstein lives in London.

* * *

Жизнь моя — черновик,
На котором все буквы —
Созвездья.
Сочтены наперед
Все ненастные дни.
Жизнь моя — черновик.
Все удачи мои, невезенья
Остаются на нем,
Как надорванный
Выстрелом крик.

1983

КТО Я?

Глазами чьими я смотрю на мир?
Друзей, родных, зверей, деревьев, птиц?
Губами чьими я ловлю росу
С листа, опавшего на мостовую?

Руками чьими обнимаю мир,
Который так беспомощен, непрочен?
Свой голос я теряю в голосах
Лесов, полей, дождей, метелей, ночи.

Но кто же я?
В чем мне искать себя?
Ответить как
Всем голосам природы?

1982

*　　*　　*

All the letters of this jotted draft
which is my life
are like a scatter of stars
All the bad days that lie ahead
are fixed in advance

All my successes and my failures
lie there, fixed,
each one like a shot
or else a scream cut short.

1983   (E.F.)

WHO AM I?

Whose are the eyes I look through at the world
of friends and family, of trees and birds?
Whose are the lips I use to catch the dew
from a leaf that has fallen in the street?

Whose are the arms I use to hug
this helpless and precarious world?
I lose my own voice in those of forests,
fields and blizzards, heavy rain and night.

But who am I?
Where should I look for myself?
How can I answer
all these natural voices?

1982   (E.F.)

* * *

Я стою у черты,
Где кончается
Связь со вселенной.
Здесь разводят мосты
Ровно в полночь —
То время бессменно.

Я стою у черты —
Ну, шагни,
И окажешься сразу бессмертна.

Оглянулась — за мною дни,
Что дарили мне столько света.

И я
Сделать последний шаг
Не могу.
Но торопит время.
Утром меркнет моя звезда
И черта обернулась мгновеньем.

1983

МЕЖДУГОРОДНЫЕ ЗВОНКИ

Междугородные звонки,
Вы с богом наперегонки.
Вокруг планеты —
Кто кого?

*   *   *

I am standing at the edge of the universe,
the line where it ends
The bridge of that connection
is drawn up at midnight exactly
the time is inflexible.

I stand on that edge
invited to step over
and become immortal.
As I look back, I see days
behind me which gave me so much light

So I
cannot
take the final step.
But time hurries me.
In the morning my star will dim,
and the line be folded in a moment.

1983   (E.F.)

LONG DISTANCE CALLS

Long distance calls
are in a race with God
all around the planet —
who can win it?

От криков лопнуло стекло,
Которое меж ним и мной.
Долой звонки,
Звонки долой.

Мы будем молча говорить,
Глаза — в глаза,
Чтоб сохранить
Больной от воплей
Шар земной.
Пусть он зашелестит травой,
И ветер закружит листвой
Над раненой моей землей.
...Мы будем молча говорить
О том,
Как детство не убить.

1983

ХОЧУ ДОБРА

Как часто
Я ловлю косые взгляды.
И колкие слова
Как стрелы
Вонзаются в меня.
Я вас прошу — послушайте!
Не надо
Губить во мне
Минуты
Детских снов.
Так невелик
Мой день,
Я так хочу добра
Всем,

Your noise breaks through the glass
between the Lord and me.
I'm finished with such calls,
finished with calls!

I'll speak to Him in silence
(only our eyes meeting)
of how to save the earth
that is so sick of shouting.
And as the grass is rustled,
and leaves swirl in the wind
over my wounded earth,
we will speak in silence
of how not
to kill childhood.

1983   (E.F.)

I WANT KINDNESS

How often
I catch sidelong glances
and sharp words hurt me
like arrows
I implore you — listen! You must not
destroy the shortlived
childlike dreams in me.
My day is so small,
and I want kindness
so much
for everyone

И даже тем,
Кто целится
В меня.

1983

ГАДАНЬЕ

Гадают сейчас
На времени,
Карты ушли в историю.
Кому выпадает черная —
Бросают туда бомбу.
Не карты,
А люди раскинуты
На бедном
Земном шаре,
И каждый боится вытащить
Кровью залитые страны.

Как жаль, что
Я не гадалка,
Гадала бы
Только цветами
И радугой залечила
Земле нанесенные
Раны.

1983

even those
who aim
at me.

1983   (E.F.)

TELLING FORTUNES

Nowadays people tell fortunes
with time,
cards are history now.
Getting a black one means
getting bombed.
Not a deck of cards,
but people are scattered
over the poor
globe,
everyone afraid of picking
a blood-stained country.
What a shame that
I'm not a fortune teller.
I would tell fortunes
only with flowers
and I would heal
the earth's wounds
with a rainbow.

1983   (A.B.)

* * *

Тяжелы мои стихи —
Камни в гору.
Донесу их до скалы,
До упору.
Упаду лицом в траву,
Слез не хватит.
Разорву свою строфу —
Стих заплачет.
Болью врежется в ладонь
Крапива́!
Превратится горечь дня
Вся в слова.

1981

ТАМ, ГДЕ ГРОХОЧЕТ ВОЙНА

Слепой ребенок
На куче хлама
Играл осколками стекла.
И в мертвых его глазах
Стояло солнце,
Не виданное им.
И блики мерцали
На колких стеклышках,
И пальцы, дрожа,
Перерывали мусор,

*   *   *

My poems are heavy,
hauling rocks uphill.
I'll carry them to the cliff,
its sheer, blank face.
I'll fall face down into the grass,
I won't have enough tears.
I'll tear up my line —
the verse will weep.
Nettles
will dig pain into my hand!
And the bitterness of the day
will all be transformed into words.

1981   (A.B.)

WHERE WAR THUNDERS

A blind child
on a mound of rubble
played with shards of glass.
And in his dead eyes
stood the sun
unseen by him.
And reflections shimmered
on the sharp pieces of glass,
and his fingers, trembling,
dug through the rubble,

Думая, что это
Цветы,
Растущие под небом
Рая.
Слепой ребенок
Радовался утру,
Не зная
И не ведая, что ночь
Всегда стоит
За детскими
Его плечами.

1983

* * *

Мы говорим с тобой
На разных языках.
Все буквы те же,
А слова чужие.
Живем с тобой
На разных островах,
Хотя в одной квартире.

1983

thinking that they were
flowers,
growing under the sky
of paradise.
The blind child
delighted in morning,
not knowing
not aware that it was
always night,
behind his
boyish shoulders.

1983   (A.B.)

*   *   *

We speak a different language,
you and I.
The script may be the same,
but the words are strange.
You and I
live on different
islands, even though
we are in the same apartment.

1983   (E.F.)

* * *

Дождь, ночь, разбитое окно.
И осколки стекла
Застряли в воздухе,
Как листья,
Не подхваченные ветром.
Вдруг — звон...
Точно так же
Обрывается жизнь человека.

1981

ОДНОМУ СЛУШАТЕЛЮ

«Я вам почитаю стихи...»
В глазах недоверия
Черные точки.
И я убегаю,
Как раненый кочет
По тонкому,
Зыбкому льду.

1983

*   *   *

Rain, night, a broken window
and shards of glass
stuck up in the air
like leaves the wind does not pick up.

Suddenly, there is a sound of ringing . . .
That is exactly how
a human life breaks off.

1981   (E.F.)

TO A CERTAIN LISTENER

'I'll read my poems to you . . .'
I offer, and then see those
black dots of distrust in your eyes.
And run away,
as a wounded bird does
on thin
fragile ice.

1983   (E.F.)

ОСТАНОВИСЬ НА МИГ

Зачем,
Когда придет пора,
Мы гоним детство со двора?
Зачем стараемся скорей
Перешагнуть ступени дней?
Спешим расти.

И годы все
Мы пробегаем,
Как во сне.
Остановись на миг!
Смотри,
Забыли мы поднять
С земли
Мечты об алых парусах,
О сказках,
Ждущих нас впотьмах.
Я по ступенькам,
Как по дням,
Сбегу к потерянным годам.
Я детство на руки возьму
И жизнь свою верну ему.

1983

СМЫСЛ ЖИЗНИ

Ступеньки вверх,
Ступеньки вниз —
Кружится голова.
Ступеньки вверх,

STOP FOR AN INSTANT

Why,
when the time comes,
do we chase childhood out of the door?
Why do we try
to skip over the steps of days?
We hurry to grow up.
And we run
past all the years,
as if in a dream.
Stop for an instant!
Look,
we forgot to pick up
from the ground
dreams of red sails,
of fairy tales,
waiting for us in the dark.
I will run down the steps,
as if they were days,
to my lost years.
I will pick up childhood in my arms
and return my life to it.

1983   (A.B.)

THE MEANING OF LIFE

Steps up,
steps down —
My head spins.
Steps up,

Ступеньки вниз —
Как жизнь моя мала!
Но не хочу
Я верить в то,
Что смерть придет ко мне,
Что не увижу никогда
Я снега в январе,
Весной
Я не сорву цветов
И не сплету венок.

Прошу!
Не надо лишних слов,
А просто верьте в то,
Что утром снова день придет
И будете опять
Ступеньки вверх,
Ступеньки вниз,
Летя по ним, считать.

1981

* * *

За что
Мы бросаем
Сухие цветы
Прошедшими днями
На мостовую.
К киоску подходим
И тут же — другую

steps down —
how small my life is!
But I do not want
to believe that
death will come to me.
That I will never see
snow in January,
in spring
I will not pick flowers
and weave a wreath.
Please!
No excess words,
simply believe that
day will come again in the morning,
and that once again
you will fly along
steps up,
steps down,
and count them.

1981   (A.B.)

*   *   *

Why do we
toss away
withered flowers
on to the street?
Because at a kiosk,
we can buy ourselves new beauty
for a rouble immediately.

За рубль покупаем себе красоту.
Бросаем   друзей.
Что было вчера,
Спешим позабыть —
Лишь бы не было больно,
И ненависть я
Выпускаю   на   волю —
Ловите кто хочет,
Она не моя.

1983

ДВОЙНИК

Может быть,
В завтрашнем дне,
В мире ином,
Приду на свиданье
Со своим двойником.
Он отраженье мое,
Невысказанные слова.
Он боль моя
И беда моя.
Слеза непросохшая на моей щеке —
Его слеза.
Его больные глаза —
Мои глаза.
Я вытащу зеркало,
Оно разбито мной.
Его отраженье
Осталось во мне самой.

1983

So we abandon friends
and hurry to forget
what happened
yesterday,
(as long as we aren't hurt)
we can express our hatred:
whoever wants it
can catch it.
It isn't mine!

1983   (E.F.)

THE DOUBLE

In tomorrow's day, perhaps,
in another world
I'll keep an appointment
with my double.
He is my reflection,
my unspoken words.
He is my bad luck
and my suffering.
The tear on my cheek,
undried, belongs to him.
His sorrowful eyes
are my eyes.
Now let me pull out my mirror.
Let me break it.
His reflection
still remains in me.

1983   (E.F.)

* * *

Уезжаю, уезжаю
Я от шума городского,
И за окнами вагона
Пробегают тополя,
Расстаются только в книгах,
Я же встречи ожидаю,
Даже если мне вернуться
Не придется никогда.

1983

* * *

Вы — поводырь,
А я — слепой старик.
Вы — проводник.
Я — еду без билета.
И мой вопрос
Остался без ответа,
И втоптан в землю
Прах друзей моих.
Вы — глас людской.
Я — позабытый стих.

1983

*　　*　　*

I'm leaving, I'm leaving
the noise of the city
and past the train windows
the poplars run by.
No one is parting,
that's bookish, I'm hoping
for meetings to come
if I never go back.

1983 (E.F.)

FOR YEVGENY YEVTUSHENKO

You are a guide
and I an old blind man.
You are a conductor
and I'm travelling without a ticket.
And my question
is unanswered.
And the remains of my friends
are ground into dirt.
You are the people's voice.
I am a forgotten verse.

1983 (A.B.)

* * *

Информация человечества
Собирается в слове
«Вечность».
Вечен свет,
Если ночь его
Не убьет.
Вечен мир,
Если смертью
Не разорвет
Шар земной.
Он прозрачен
И чист,
Как январский снег...

Пожалей его,
Человек.
Пожалей свой дом,
Он частичка твоя,
Сын твой там
Или дочь —
Это тоже земля.

Информация человечества
Обрывается только
Вечностью.

1983

*   *   *

The information of humanity
is collected in the word
'eternity.'
Light is eternal,
if night
doesn't kill it.
The world is eternal,
if death
doesn't blow up
the world.
It is transparent
and pure
like January snow. . .

Pity it,
mankind.
Pity your house,
it is part of you,
your son is there,
or your daughter —
that is also the world.

The information of humanity
is cut off only by
eternity.

1983   (A.B.)

* * *

Благослови меня, строка,
Благослови мечом и раной.
Я упаду,
Но тут же
Встану.
Благослови меня,
Строка.

1983

* * *

Как трудно стало
Мне писать,
По сердцу
Барабанят дробью
Слова,
Кому мне их сказать?
Птенцом
Попала я в неволю.
И клетка
Очень хороша,

Вода и корм —
Всего там вдоволь.
Но ключ от моего ларца
Семью печатями окован.
Хозяин мой
Бывает добр,

*   *   *

Bless me, line,
bless me with sword and wound.
I will fall,
but get up
right away.
Bless me,
line.

1983   (A.B.)

*   *   *

How hard it is
for me to write,
words
drum a roll
upon my heart,
to whom can I say them?
As a fledgling
I was caught.
And the cage
is very nice,
there is lots
of food and water.
But the key to my coffer
is hidden away. . .
My master
is sometimes kind,

И дверцу
На ночь открывает,
Но сторожем
Он оставляет
Тьму
За невымытым окном.

1983

НУЛИ

Я научусь считать до 10, 30, 100,
И еще очень много нулей...
А что будет потом?
Я останусь маленькой
И шепотом расскажу
Маме сказку
О Красной Шапочке
И о том,
Что бывает страшно
Не только ночью,
Но и днем,
Потому, что я боюсь цифр,
В которых много нулей.
Они так похожи
На пасти жутких
Диких зверей.

1982

and opens the door
at night,
but on guard duty
he leaves
the dark
outside the unwashed window.

1983   (A.B.)

ZEROS

I will learn to count to 10, 30, 100,
and many other zeros. . .
And then what will happen?
I will still be small
and in a whisper tell
Mama a story
about Little Red Riding Hood
and that
it can be scary
not only at night,
but in the daytime,
because I am afraid of numbers
with many zeros.
They look so much
like the jaws of
horrible wild animals.

1982   (A.B.)

СОЛОВЕЙ

Заслоню плечом тяжесть дня
И оставлю вам соловья.
И оставлю вам только ночь,
Чем могу я еще помочь?
А хотите, я сердце отдам —
Пусть судьба моя пополам.
Даже время умрет до утра,
Но проспали вы соловья.
Торопясь, вместо сердца
Вы взяли часы.
День пришел,
Слышишь, ночь, ты его не ищи.

1983

ТРИ ТЮЛЬПАНА

Е. Камбуровой

Три кровавые слезы,
Три тюльпана.
Молча женщина сидит.
От дурмана
Закружилась голова,
Сжалось сердце.

THE NIGHTINGALE

I can block the hardship of the day
with my shoulder, and leave you a nightingale,
and leave you only the night.

What else can I do for you?
If you want, I'll give you my heart
and share my fate equally.
Before morning, even time may stop.

But you slept through the nightingale.
You were in such a hurry
you preferred a watch to my heart,
and now it's daytime, listen:

Don't go looking for the night.

1983   (E.F.)

THREE TULIPS

for E. Kamburova

Three bloody tears of
three tulips.
A woman silently sits.
Intoxication
made her head spin,
her heart contracts.

Три тюльпана
Получила ты в наследство.
Только ветер прошумел:
«Быть им ложью!»
Но глаза твои кричат:
«Быть не может!»
Три тюльпана, три слезы
Облетели.
Молча женщина сидит,
Им не веря.

1983

* * *

Я ночь люблю за одиночество,
Когда с собой наедине
Я говорю о том,
Что хочется
И что не хочется судьбе.
Могу я думать о несбыточном,
О том,
Что ночи нет конца.
И можно верить
В дни счастливые,
И плакать можно без конца.
Не надо слушать слов укора.
И глаз тревожных острие
Не надо прикрывать рукою,
Когда становится темно.

1982

Three tulips
you inherited.
Only the wind rustled:
'Lies they be!'
But your eyes scream:
'It can't be!'
Three tulips, three tears
fell off.
Silently the woman sits,
not believing them.

1983   .B.)

*   *   *

It is the solitude of night I love
being alone
on my own.
I talk about
whatever I want then,
and everything that fate doesn't allow.
I can think about
altogether impossible things:
such as a night which has no end.
Believe in happy days,
or weep for as long as I like.
And I don't have to cover up
the sharpness of anxious eyes
when the light goes.

1982   (E.F.)

* * *

Не пишутся мои стихи,
Ни слова и ни строчки.
Разбросаны, как городки,
Все запятые, точки.

И день закончился без снов.
И ночь пройдет в потемках.
Ушли стихи, как тает лед
От солнца на пригорке.

Но трудно мне дышать без слов —
Все улицы узки.
Искать я пробую слова —
Дороги коротки.

Все перепутаны пути,
Дождями рифмы смыты.
И даже буквы в букваре
Все мною позабыты.

Не пишутся мои стихи,
Нет больше боли и тоски.

1981

*   *   *

My poem isn't writing well,
neither words nor lines.
The commas and the stops
scatter like skittles.

The day ended without dreams.
And the night will pass in twilight.
The poems are gone, like ice
melting on the hill.

But it is hard for me to breathe without words —
all the streets are narrow.
I try to find the words —
but the roads are too short.

All the paths are jumbled,
the rains have washed away the rhymes.
And I've even forgotten all
the letters in my primer.

My poem isn't writing well,
there is no more pain and sorrow.

1981   (A.B.)

ВОЗВРАЩЕНЬЕ

Каблучки по ступенькам,
В дверь звонок.
Ты стоишь —
За плечами взмах волос.
И распахнуты руки,
Как разорвана ночь.
Я не верю в разлуку,
Все слезы прочь.
Но ты смотришь
С тревогой,
Снова дни пролистав.
По железной дороге
Не вернулся состав.

Ты осталась
В том доме,
Где чужие углы.
Где все лица в разломе,
Где молчанье
Как крик.
И уколешься взглядом
О чужие слова.
Лифт захлопнется рядом,
Ты ему не нужна...
Этажи бесконечны,
И в проеме окон
Будет лиц бессердечье,
Как церковный звон.

1982

THE RETURN

Your heels sound on the steps
there is a ring at the door.
And there you stand,
your hair surging behind you,
your arms flung wide open,
as night is torn open.
And I don't believe
in separation,
let's have no more tears.
You look afraid
as you flip through the days you've lived.

The train did not come back
along the track.
You remained
in a house
of unfamiliar corners,
where all the faces are shattered
where there is silence
and also much shouting.
And there your gaze
will be pricked by another person's words.
Nearby a lift will slam shut.
He doesn't need you.
What endless stories!
And at every window
indifferent faces
like the ringing of church bells.

1982   (E.F.)

УРОНИЛА В РУКИ ВОЛОСЫ

Уронила в руки волосы —
Как пшеничная вода.
А напьешься —
Вмиг накатится
Серебристая волна.
Время горького дыханье
Подступило, не унять.
Как трава еще не вялая,
Только стоит ли срывать?
Завтра по утру оглянешься —
Вышел год.
Уронила в руки волосы —
Твои черед.

1983

* * *

Как больно, помогите,
В глазах беда.
Но годы-паутинки
Растают без следа.
Рукой не обопрешься —
Душа пуста.
По волчьим тропам бродит
Моя звезда.

1983

WHEN YOU DROP YOUR HAIR

When you drop your hair into your hands
it is like a stream of wheat,
and when you are drunk
it is like watching
a silver wave breaking.
Now is a time of bitter breathing
there is no avoiding it.
The grass has not yet faded.
Is it worth pulling it up?
Tomorrow morning, as you look around,
a year will have gone by.
You drop your hair into your hands.
Now it is your move!

1983   E.F.)

*   *   *

It hurts so much, help,
trouble in my eyes.
But the cobweb years
will dissolve without a trace.
You can't lean on your arm —
the soul is empty.
My star wanders
down wolf tracks.

1983   (A.B.)

Я ДОМ УБЕРУ

Я дом уберу
И мебель поставлю
В пустые углы.
Вымою пол,
Почищу ковры
И сяду.
За стеклами
Дождик запляшет,
И день одиночеством
Страшным накажет.
Как хочется мне
Обойти стороной
Калитку, и сад,
И цветущий левкой.
Но каждое утро
Я день начинаю
В том доме,
И пыль вытираю,
И окна от ветра
Закрою.

1983

КОСУ ЗАПЛЕТИ ТУГУЮ

Косу заплети тугую,
Улицей пройди
И услышишь
За собою
Гулкие шаги.

I WILL CLEAN THE HOUSE

I will clean the house
and put the furniture
in empty corners.
I will wash the floor
and fix the rugs,
and then sit down.
Behind the window panes
the rain will splash
and the day will punish me
with horrible loneliness.
I want so much
to go around the gate
and into the garden,
so I can look at all the flowers there.
But every morning instead
I start the day dusting,
and shutting the windows
against the wind.

1983   (E.F.)

BRAID YOUR HAIR TIGHTLY

Braid your hair tightly
and go down the street
and you'll hear
resounding steps
behind you.

Это — время,
Что хотела
Ты забыть.
Не надейся,
Этой встрече
Непременно быть.
И ты знаешь,
Расплатиться
Ты должна
За слова,
Что были сказаны
Тогда.
Веришь,
Время перепутает пути,
И поэтому
Ты
Косу не плети.

1983

* * *

Убаюкайте меня, укачайте
И укройте потеплей одеялом.
Колыбельной песней обманите,
Сны свои мне утром подарите.
Дни с картинками,

That is time,
which you wanted
to forget.
Stop hoping,
the meeting
is inevitable.
And you know,
you must
pay
for the words
that were said
then,
believe,
time will cross the paths,
and that is why
you
shouldn't braid your hair.

1983   (A.B.)

*   *   *

Sing me a lullaby, rock me
to sleep, cover me with a blanket:
deceive me with your lulling,
give me your dreams in the morning.

On some days the image of
the sun is bluer than ice,

Где солнце голубее льда,
Под подушку утром положите.
Но не ждите, слышите,
Не ждите,
Детство убежало от меня.

1982

* * *

Душа-невидимка,
Где ты живешь?
Твой маленький домик,
Наверно, хорош?
Ты бродишь по городу,
Бродишь одна,
Душа-невидимка,
Ты мне не видна.

1983

НОВОСТИ ДНЯ

Я жду,
Когда кто-нибудь
Спросит меня,
Что видела, виделась с кем,
Где была.
Тогда я открою альбом новостей,
Вам хочется новых
Услышать вестей?

put that under my pillow
in the morning, but don't wait,

listen, don't wait.
Childhood has run away from me.

1982   (E.F.)

*   *   *

Where are you living now
invisible soul?
Your tiny home
must be lovely.
You are wandering
alone in the city
invisible soul
and I can't see you.

1983   E.F.)

NEWS OF THE DAY

I am waiting for someone to ask me
what have I seen, whom have I seen
and where have I been?
Then I shall open up my album.

Кто умер, уехал,
Остался один...
А можно,
Мы просто
Чуть-чуть помолчим?
Увидим последний
Трамвай за окном...
Я очень люблю засыпающий дом.
И пылью покроются
Новости дня.
И я понимаю —
Не ждали меня.

1983

* * *

Каждый человек
Ищет свой путь.
Но все равно
Попадает на ту дорогу,
По краям которой
Стоят жизнь и смерть.
Я бы дольше
Хотела идти
По той стороне,
Где не заходит солнце.
Но за днем
Всегда наступает ночь,
Поэтому
Я ищу тропинки.

1983

You want to hear new gossip?
Who's died, who's gone away,
who's been abandoned . . .
Let's say nothing for a bit.
Until we see the last trolley
through the window . . .
I like a house as it's falling asleep.
Dust will cover up
the news of the day.
And then I understand.
It wasn't me they were waiting for.

1983   (E.F.)

*   *   *

Every person
seeks his path.
But nevertheless
he gets on the road
with life and death
standing on the shoulder.
I would like
to walk longer
on the side
where the sun does not set.
But every day
is followed by night.
That's why
I'm looking for a lane.

1983   (A.B.)

ДОМ ПАСТЕРНАКА

Сад, терраса.
На ступенях
Желтый лист.
Окна смотрят
В темноту.
Слышен лишь
Тайный голос.
Он по клавишам
Бродил
Всю ночь.
Голос этот
Так хотел помочь.
Время прошлое
И новое
Собрать у старых
Стен.
Только этот дом
Не любит перемен.
Ночь уйдет.
А утром клавиши молчат.
Только голоса
В душе кричат.

1983

PASTERNAK'S HOUSE

Garden, terrace.
On the steps
a yellow leaf.
The windows look out
into darkness.
Only a secret
voice is heard.
It wandered
over the keyboard
all night.
That voice
wanted to help.
To collect
times past
and new from the old
walls.
Only this house
doesn't like changes.
Night will go away.
And in the morning the keys are silent.
But voices
shout in my soul.

1983   (A.B.)

БАБУШКЕ

Я печаль твою развею,
Соберу букет цветов.
Постараюсь, как сумею,
Написать немного слов
О рассвете ранне-синем,
О весеннем соловье.
Я печаль твою развею,
Только непонятно мне,
Почему, оставшись дома,
Сердце болью защемит.
От стены и до порога
Путь тревогою разбит.
И букет цветов завянет —
В доме пе живут цветы.
Я печаль твою развею,
Станешь счастлива ли ты?

1982

ФОКУСНИК

А. Акопяну

Поднимите пальцы-нервы,
Превратите гроздь рябины
В брызги моря,
Что шумело за окном,
Тревожно вторя
Вечной тайне сна и были.

TO GRANDMOTHER

Let me disperse your sorrow.
I shall gather a bouquet of flowers,
I will try as hard as I can to write
a few words about the early blue
of sunrise, and the spring nightingale.
Let me disperse your sorrow.
If only I could understand
why staying at home
makes my heart ache with pain.
The path is broken with worry
between the wall and the threshold
And the bouquet will wither
because flowers don't live in this house.
Let me disperse your sorrow —
But will that make you happy?

1982   (E.F.)

MAGICIAN

for A. Akopyan

Lift your nerve-fingers,
turn a cluster of rowanberries
into the spray of the sea
that roared outside the window
anxiously seconding
the eternal mystery of sleep and the past.

Превратите листьев стаю
В дерзкий клекот журавлиный.
Раскачайте на качелях
Ветер,
Превращенный в иней.
Помогите мне запомнить
Все раздумья и сомненья.
Дайте руку!
Я хотела б
Сердца ощутить биенье.

1982

* * *

Срубленные рифмы,
Срубленные фразы,
Срублены деревья —
Повалили лес.
Стон стоит,
Отчаянно
В плаче рвутся ветви.
Но и мало этого —
Листья подожгли!
Не пишитесь, строки,
Иль пишитесь в небе.
Ведь бумага кровью
Вся обагрена.

1983

Turn the flock of leaves
into the brazen call of cranes.
Swing the wind,
turned into hoarfrost,
in a swing.
Help me remember
all my thoughts and doubts.
Give me your hand!
I would like to feel
heartbeats.

1982   (A.B.)

*   *   *

Chopped rhymes,
chopped phrases,
chopped trees —
the forest is felled.
Moans rise,
desperately
trees sway and weep.
But that's not enough —
they've set fire to the leaves!
Lines — don't be written,
or be written in the sky.
For the paper is becrimsoned
with blood.

1983   (A.B.)

ОДНОЙ ИЗ ЖЕНЩИН

В шесть сорок
Отбудет поезд.
В шесть сорок
Наступит расплата
За то, что
Забыла вернуться,
Что смех у тебя
На лице.
Ты выйдешь на станцию.
Тихо.
Твой поезд
Ушел на рассвете.
Не надо
Придумывать фразы,
Чтоб время простило тебя.
Ты просто забыла о дате,
Уходит нескорый поезд.
В шесть сорок
Приедет любимый,
Но это было вчера.

1983

TO ONE OF THE WOMEN

At six forty
the train will leave.
At six forty
retribution
for forgetting
to return,
for the laughter
on your face.
You will come to the station
quietly.
Your train
left at dawn.
Don't
make up phrases,
for time to forgive you.
You simply forgot the date,
the slow train is leaving.
At six forty
your beloved will come,
but that was yesterday.

1983 (A.B.)

РАНЕНАЯ ПТИЦА

Пожалейте меня, отпустите.
Крылья раненые не вяжите,
Я уже не лечу.
Голос мой оборвался болью,
Голос мой превратился в рану.
Я уже не кричу.
Помогите мне, подождите!
Осень.
Птицы летят на юг.
Только сердце сожмется страхом,
Одиночество — смерти друг.

1983

ДЕНЬ ЗАЧЕРКНУТ

День зачеркнут.
Все страницы
Будут собраны в сомненья.
День зачеркнут.
Отзовитесь
Все, кто канули в неверье,
Все, кто дымкой запоздалой
Были от меня укрыты.

WOUNDED BIRD

Have pity on me, let me go,
don't tie my wounded wings.
I can no longer fly.
My voice is broken with the pain
my voice is turned into a wound
I am no longer crying.
Help me,
Autumn
hold back a little longer.
The birds are flying South
without me now, and the only muscle of mine
that contracts is my frightened heart.

Loneliness is a friend of death.

1983   (E.F.)

THE DAY IS CROSSED OFF

The day is crossed off.
All the pages
will be collected in doubts.
The day is crossed off.
Respond,
all who plunged into disbelief,
all who by a belated haze
were hidden from me.

Отзовитесь!
Слышен еле
Поезда гудок охриплый.
Все дороги словом смыты,
Перепутаны тропинки.
Отзовитесь, дни былые,
Что звенели звонью зыбкой.
Только ветер странно воет,
Перекрестки все сметая.
Я сама страниц сомненья
Зачеркну, не понимая.

1982

МАМЕ

Мне не хватает
Нежности твоей,
Как умирающей
Птице воздуха.
Мне не хватает
Тревожного дрожанья
Губ твоих.
Когда одиноко мне,
Не хватает смешинок
В твоих глазах,
Они плачут,
Смотря на меня.
Почему в этом мире
Такая черная боль?
Наверное, оттого,
Что ты одна.

1981

Respond!
Barely audible
is the train's hoarse horn.
All the roads are washed away by words,
the paths jumbled.
Bygone days respond,
you who rang with trembling ring.
Only the wind howls strangely
blowing over all the crossroads.
I will cross out the pages of doubts
without understanding.

1982   (A.B.)

TO MAMA

I need your tenderness
as a dying bird
needs air.
I need the worried tremble
of your lips.
And when I feel lonely
I need the sparkling laughter in your eyes.
But they weep,
as they watch me.
Why is there so much black
pain in the world?
It must be because
you are alone.

1981   (E.F.)

* * *

Друзей ищу,
Я растеряла их.
Слова ищу —
Они ушли с друзьями.
Я дни ищу...
Как быстро убегали
Они вослед
Идущим от меня!

1982

ЛИЦА

Бывают такие лица,
В которых даже за полночь
В глазах остаются блики
От восходящего солнца.
Шагаю дорогой пыльной,
Гудят усталые ноги.
Но верю я в эти лица,
И делают их не боги.

1983

*　　*　　*

I search for friends,
for I have lost them.
I search for words —
they're off with my friends.
I search for days . . .
How quickly they run
after those fleeing me!

1982　　　　　　　　　　　　　　　　　　(A.B.)

FACES

There are faces
in whose eyes even after midnight
there are still reflections
of the rising sun.
I stride down the dusty road,
my tired legs ache.
But I believe in those faces
and they are made not by gods.

1983　　　　　　　　　　　　　　　　　　(A.B.)

ВОСПОМИНАНЬЕ

Я хочу с тобой одной
Посидеть у дома старого,
Дом стоит тот над рекой,
Что зовут воспоминаньем.
След ноги твоей босой
Пахнет солнцем
Лета прошлого.
Где бродили мы с тобой
По траве, еще не кошенной.
Голубели небеса,
Исчезая за околицей,
И звенели голоса,
Вот и все,
Что мне запомнилось.
И отсчет всех дней
Подошел к концу.
Стаей птиц
Все дни
Собрались у ног.
Покормить их чем?
Не осталось строк...

1981

REMEMBRANCE

I want to sit alone with you
I want to sit alone
near the old house,
the house that stands
by the river of memory.
The print of your bare foot
smells of last Summer's sun.
Where you and I wandered
on the still unmown grass.
The skies were blue,
and disappeared beyond the outskirts.
Voices rang out
and that's all I remember.
The accounting of the days
has reached an end.
Like a flock of birds
all the days
have gathered at our feet.
I don't know what to feed them,
there are no lines left.

1981   (E.F.)

ГОЛОС

По аллеям парка
Шариком хрустальным
Голос твой звенящий
Обогнал меня.

Пробежал по крышам,
Пробежал по листьям,
В шорохе осеннем
Музыку поймал.

Вдруг остановился
Возле той скамейки,
Где стоял разбитый
Уличный фонарь.

Шарик твой хрустальный
Заискрился смехом.
И фонарь разбитый
Вдруг светиться стал.

1981

* * *

Не слушайте уличных фонарей —
Они укладывают спать.
Забудьте грусть.
Наступит час,

THE VOICE

Down the parkway
like a crystal ball
your ringing voice
passed me.

It ran along rooftops,
it ran along leaves,
in the autumnal rustle
it captured music.

Suddenly, it stopped
near the bench,
with the smashed
lamp post.

Your crystal ball
sparkled with laughter.
And the smashed lamp post
suddenly glowed light.

1981   (A.B.)

*   *   *

Don't listen to lamp posts.
They send you to sleep.
Put aside sorrow.
The time will come

Когда уйдет беда, печаль
И звезды позовут к себе.
Не слушайте уличных фонарей —
Они укладывают спать.

1981

УЛИЦА

Убегает улица
Вверх.
И поймать ее — просто
Смех.
Побегу я за ней
Вдаль.
Оглянусь вдруг назад —
Жаль.
Жаль оставленный мной
Дом,
Маму, плачущую за окном.
Плеск волны у меня
За спиной,
Лай собаки, бегущей
За мной.
Убегай-ка, улица,
Ты одна.
Ведь тебе-то
Я не нужна.

1980

when sadness and ill luck will cease
and the stars will call you to them.
Don't listen to lamp posts.
They send you to sleep.

1981   (E.F.)

THE STREET

The street runs
up.
Catching it is just a
joke.
I'll run after it
far.
I'll look back —
sorry.
Sorry to leave my
house,
Mother, crying in the window.
Wave splashing
behind me,
bark of the dog running
after me.
Street, run off
by yourself.
After all,
you don't need me.

1980   (A.B.)

ЛОЖЬ

«Ты нам нахально лжешь», —
Все говорят вокруг.
Но врут они,
Не ведая, не зная,
Что ложь моя
Сложилась из трамвая,
Который вдруг
Увез меня в страну,
Неведомую вам,
Увез из шороха намокнувшей листвы,
Которая дрожит тревожно
На тонком дереве у дома.
Из лиц,
Которые порой
Бывают одиноки страшно.
Из речки,
Вдруг разбуженной,
Потоком гремящих вод.
Из маленькой девчонки,
Которая все не находит дома.
Из веры, что порой
Для многих
Пахнет ложью.

1981

LIE

'You keep lying to us' —
everyone around me says.
But they're the ones who lie,
not knowing
that my lie
consists of the trolley
which suddenly
took me to a country
unknown to you,
took me from the rustle of damp leaves,
that tremble anxiously
on the thin tree by my house.
Of faces,
which sometimes
are terribly lonely.
Of a river,
which is awakened
by the flood of roaring waters.
Of a little girl,
who still is lost.
Of the faith which sometimes
for many
smells of lies.

1981   (A.B.)

* * *

По гулким лестницам
Я поднимаюсь к дому,
Как ключ тяжел,
Я дверь им отопру.
Так страшно,
Но иду безвольно
И попадаю сразу в темноту.
Включаю свет,
Но вместо света лижет
Меня огонь,
Палящий и живой.
Я отраженья в зеркале
Не вижу —
Подернуто оно
Печальной пеленой.
Окно хочу открыть —
Стекло, смеясь
И холодом звеня,
Отбрасывает
В сторону меня.
И я кричу,
От боли сводит щеки,
Слеза бежит
Сквозь сонные глаза.
И слышу шепот,
Тихий мамин шепот:
«Проснись, родная,
Не пугайся зря».

1983

*　　*　　*

Up echoing steps
I ascend to the house —
how heavy the key is,
I'll open the door.
How scary,
but I go unwillingly
and end up in darkness.
I turn on the light,
but instead of the light
fire licks me,
blazing and alive.
I don't see my reflection
in the mirror —
it is covered
with a sad film.
I want to open the window —
the glass, laughing
and ringing with cold,
tosses
me aside.
And I shout,
my cheeks contorted with pain,
a tear runs through
sleepy eyes.
I hear a whisper —
Mother's quiet whisper —
'Wake up, darling,
don't be afraid in vain.'

1983   (A.B.)

ДЕНЬ РОЖДЕНЬЯ

Нечаянно я забыла
День рожденья своего.
А может быть, нарочно не хочу
Я часовую стрелку повернуть
Обратно в детство.
Боюсь я потерять
Ту тайну жизни,
Что бережно мне
Отдавали люди,
Забыв себя...

Сломав цветок,
Не вырастишь его.
Убив ручей,
Воды ты не напьешься,
Я семь ступеней
Жизни прохожу,
Но не могу понять,
Которая из них —
Мой день рожденья.

1981

BIRTHDAY

I accidentally forget
the day of my birth.
Or maybe, it was on purpose
I don't want to turn the clock hand
back into childhood.
I'm afraid to lose
that secret of life
which was carefully given me
by people,
who forgot themselves . . .

If you break a flower,
you won't grow it.
If you kill a brook,
you won't get a drink.
I'm passing the seven stages of life,
but I can't understand
which of them is
my birthday.

1981   (A.B.)

НЕ Я ПИШУ СВОИ СТИХИ?

Не я пишу свои стихи?
Ну хорошо, не я.
Не я кричу, что нет строки?
Не я.
Не я боюсь дремучих снов?
Не я.
Не я кидаюсь в бездну слов?
Ну хорошо, не я.

Вы просыпаетесь во тьме,
И нету сил кричать.
И нету слов...
Нет, есть слова!
Возьмите-ка тетрадь
И напишите вы о том,
Что видели во сне,
Что стало больно и светло,
Пишите о себе.
Тогда поверю вам, друзья,
Мои стихи пишу не я.

1982

IT'S NOT I WHO WRITES MY POEMS?

It's not I who writes my poems?
Well, all right, not I.
It's not I who cries there is no line?
Not I.
Not I who fears deep dreams?
Not I.
Not I who plunges into the abyss of words?
Well, all right, not I.

You wake up in the dark
and don't have the strength to cry out.
And there are no words . . .
No, there are words!
You take a notebook then
and write about
what you saw in your dream,
what was painful and luminous,
write about yourselves.
Then I'll believe you, my friends,
that it is not I who writes my poems.

1982   (A.B.)

* * *

Я играю на рояле.
Пальцы эхом пробежали,
Им от музыки тревожно,
Больно и светло.
Я играю на рояле,
Слов не знаю,
Нот не знаю,
Только странно
Мне от звука,
Что наполнил дом.
Он распахивает окна,
В вихре закружил деревья.
Перепутал
Утро с ночью
Этот тайный звук.
Я играю на рояле,
Пальцы тихо замирают.
Это музыка вселенной —
Тесен ей мой дом.

1983

*   *   *

I play the piano.
My fingers run like echoes,
agitated by the music,
pained and luminous.
I play the piano,
I don't know the words,
I don't know the music,
only I feel strange
from the sound
that filled the house.
It flings open windows,
whipping the trees in a whirlwind.
That secret sound
confused
morning and night.
I play the piano,
My fingers softly stop.
This is the music of the universe —
my house is too cramped.

1983   (A.B.)

* * *

Так день далек,
Как ночь,
Когда гроза.
Когда глаза
Не могут видеть
Капелек дождя,
Но ловят их
Губами
У порога дома.
Как руки,
Которые не могут
В темноте найти стены
И натыкаются на двери в день,
Который так далек...

1982

* * *

Вы умеете пальцами слушать дождь?
Это просто!
Дотроньтесь рукой до коры дерева,
И она задрожит под вашими пальцами,
Как мокрый конь.
Дотроньтесь рукой
До оконного стекла ночью.
Вы слышите?
Оно боится дождя,
Но оно должно охранять меня
От мокрых капель,
Я поглажу капли пальцами
Через стекло.

*   *   *

Day is far off
like night
when there is a storm,
and no eye can
see drops of rain
only lips can catch them
at their opening,
as hands cannot find
the walls in the dark,
and bump into doors in daylight.

1982   (E.F.)

*   *   *

Do you know how to listen to the rain with your fingers?
It's easy!
Touch the bark of a tree
and it will tremble under your fingers
like a wet horse.
Touch
a window pane at night.
It is afraid of rain
and yet protects me
from the drops:
I will pet them with my fingers
through the glass.

Дождь!
Дверь!
Послушай, дверь,
Отпусти меня!
Улица полна звона ручьев.
Я хочу пальцами услышать дождь,
Чтобы потом написать музыку.

1981

МАМЕ

Я надеюсь на тебя.
Запиши все мои строчки.
А не то наступит точно
Ночь без сна.
Собери мои страницы
В толстую тетрадь.
Я потом
Их постараюсь разобрать.
Только, слышишь,
Не бросай меня одну.
Превратятся
Все стихи мои в беду.

1983

I shall cry out:
Rain!
Door!
Listen, door, let me out!
The street is full of streams.
I want to hear the rain with my fingers,
so that I can write its music.

1981   (E.F.)

TO MAMA

I depend on you
to write down my lines,
otherwise I'll certainly
have a sleepless night.
So gather my pages
into a fat notebook.
I'll try and
figure them out later.
Only listen
don't leave me alone
or all my poems
will turn into misfortune.

1983   (E.F.)

КАЛЕЙДОСКОП

Антону Ежову

Ребенок взял калейдоскоп
Глазок в глазок, и вмиг
Рассыпался
Весь безголосый мир
На разноцветный крик.
Он строит
Замки для царевен,
Зеленую луну.
Разрисовал
Весь шар земной
Оранжевой травой.
Смотри, малыш,
В твоих руках
Не только семь цветов,
Планета —
Дней калейдоскоп.
Твой взгляд —
Ее лицо.

1983

KALEIDOSCOPE

for Anton Ezhov

A child took a kaleidoscope,
eye to the eyepiece, and instantly
the whole voiceless world
shattered
into a multicoloured scream.
It builds
castles for queens,
a green moon.
It coloured
the whole globe
with orange grass.
Look, child,
in your hands
are not only seven colours.
The planet is
a kaleidoscope of days.
Your gaze
is its face.

1983   (A.B.)

* * *

М. Луговской

Вы проходите по ночи.
Сосны гулко зашептали:
«Не верпуть назад столетья
И секунду не вернуть.
Все часы замолкли разом,
Колокол гудит набатом,
Вырывается из сердца
Поминальный стон.
Подождите, не спешите,
Руку ветру протяните,
Время не для Вас.
У скалы живое сердце.
Бьется маяком надежды,
Этот свет неугасимый
Охраняет Вас».

1983

*　　*　　*

for M. Lugovskaya

You pass through the night
the pines begin whispering hollowly:
'You cannot turn back the centuries.
You cannot turn back a second.'
All the clocks grew silent at once,
the bell sounds the alarm,
a memorial moan
is torn from the heart.
Wait, do not hurry,
offer your hand to the wind,
time is not for you.
A living heart by the cliff
flutters like a lighthouse of hope.
That inextinguishable light
protects you.

1983   (A.B.)

ДОМ ПОД КАШТАНОМ

Ю. Семенову

На пыльной дороге
Изранены ноги.
Путник бредет
По пыльной дороге.
Под солнцем палящим
Вперед, и вперед, и вперед.
Рука одинока,
Подернуты болью глаза,
Слеза ли от горя,
Иль просто от ветра слеза.
Но знаю,
За морем,
В неведомом, тайном краю,
Есть дом под каштаном,
Я к этому дому иду.

1983

* * *

Я тороплюсь скорей туда,
Где ждет
Меня король.
Прошло три года
И три дня,
На сердце его боль.

THE HOUSE UNDER THE CHESTNUT TREE

for Yu. Semenov

On the dusty road
wounded legs.
A traveller wanders
down the dusty road.
Under the blazing sun,
forward, forward, forward.
The hand is alone,
rain circles the eyes,
the tear caused by sorrow
or simply by the wind.
But I know,
beyond the sea,
in an unknown, secret place
there is a house under a chestnut tree.
I am walking to that house.

1983   (A.B.)

*   *   *

I hurry
where the king
awaits me.
Three years have passed
and three days,
pain is in his heart.

И я вернулась,
А ключи
Уже не к тем замкам.
И дверь
Закрыта на засов,
И милого нет там.
Холодный ветер
В спину дул,
И слезы жгли лицо.
Он ждал три года.
Я пришла,
Забыв его лицо.

1983

Я ОБМАНУЛА ВАС

Я обманула Вас,
Что миг бывает вечность.
Что с перелетом птиц
Кончается тепло.
И позабыты мной давно
Ночей волшебных заклинанья,
Что радость так близка —
Дотронешься случайно,
Ладонь твоя
Поднимет шар земной.
Я обманула Вас?
Нет!
Подарила тайну,
Которая известна
Мне одной.

1983

I am back,
but the keys
no longer fit the locks.
The door is barred
and my beloved is not there.
A cold wind
blew at my back
and tears burned my face.
He waited three years.
I came,
having forgotten his face.

1983   (A.B.)

I FOOLED YOU

I fooled you into
believing a minute is eternity,
that when birds fly South
there's no more warmth.
And I have long ago
forgotten those incantations
of magical nights with joy so close
you can touch it by accident,
as if your hand
could lift up the world.
Did I deceive you?
No,
I gave you a secret
that is known
to me alone.

1983   (E.F.)

* * *

Я закрываю день ресницами,
Но почему-то мне не спится.
Я думаю о дне ушедшем,
Но не дошедшем
До встречи с ночью.
Об улицах, замученных людьми,
О фонарях,
Которые светить устали.
О доме том,
В котором я не сплю,
Но сон тревожной серой птицей
Подлетает вдруг ко мне
И захлопнул мне ресницы
На заре.
Просыпайся ты, малышка,
В утро-рань
И увидишь — отдохнул
Твой фонарь.
Смех заполнил перекрестки дорог,
И до вечера день далек.

1981

* * *

Птицы
Только парами
На юг летят.
Одиночкам
Крылья подрезают
Или просто молча убивают.

* * *

As my lashes close, the day ends
but I can't sleep.
I think about the passing day
which has gone by without
reaching the night,
about streets exhausted by people
and streetlights, weary
with the effort of shining
and about this house in which I can't sleep,
until sleep, an anxious grey bird,
flies up to me suddenly
at daybreak.
Now wake up, little thing,
early in the morning
and you'll see how
your streetlight has been resting,
laughter has filled the crossroads,
and a long time has gone by since evening.

1981   (E.F.)

* * *

Birds fly South
in pairs only.
Solitary birds
have their wings clipped
or are simply killed, silently.

И тревожно
Протрубит вожак.
Ты живым
Остаться хочешь, милый,
Прячешь клюв
Под белое крыло.
Осень ветром
Хмурым закружила,
А тебе
Так хочется
В тепло.

1983

* * *

Лица уходят из памяти,
Как прошлогодние листья.
Осень оставила только
Утра хмурого привкус.
Лица уходят, но изредка
К сердцу подходит холод.
Вспомнятся желтые листья.
Это как встреча с болью,
Это как встреча с прошлым,
С чьим-то портретом разбитым.
Горько от настоящего,
Страшно жить позабытым.

1983

And the leader will
honk in anxiety.
Dear, I know you
want to stay alive,
to hide your beak
under your white wing.
the Autumn
is swirling in a cold wind,
and you want so much to be
where it is warm.

1983   (E.F.)

                    *   *   *

People leave memory
like last year's leaves.
Autumn has left
only morning's grim taste.
Faces leave, but occasionally
cold strikes the heart.
Recalling yellow leaves,
is like meeting pain
is like meeting the past
with someone's broken portrait.
The present is bitter,
it is terrible to live forgotten.

1983   (A.B.)

* * *

О, как мы редко
Говорим друг другу
Надежные и нужные слова!
Поэтому найти
Так трудно друга,
Поэтому одна.

Так хочется
Дарить цветы —
Считаю потно мелочь.
Как хочется
Поджечь мосты
И позабыть,
Что надо делать.

1983

ЛОШАДИ В ПОЛЕ

Лошади в поле,
Трава высока.
Лошади в поле
Под утренним светом.
Быстро росинки бегут до рассвета,
Надо успеть напоить всю траву.
Лошади в поле,
Цокот копыт.
Тихое ржанье,

*   *   *

O, how rarely
we say dependable and needed words
to one another!
That is why it is so hard
to find a friend,
that is why I am alone.

I want badly
to give flowers —
sweatily I count the change.
I want badly
to burn bridges
and forget
what must be done.

1983   (A.B.)

HORSES IN THE MEADOW

Horses in the meadow,
the grass is tall.
Horses in the meadow
in morning light,
dewdrops quickly run before dawn,
they have to quench all of the grass.
Horses in the meadow,
hoof beats.
Quiet neighing,

Шуршанье поводьев.
Солнце, как шар,
Отплыв от земли,
Теплые пальцы
К гривам подносит.
Лошади с поля уйдут,
Но до ночи
В травах примятых
Останутся точки
От конских копыт.

1981

* * *

В. И. Николаевой

Я поверила взгляду,
И не нужны слова.
Я поверила сразу,
Что бывает слеза
Солоней боли черной,
Слаще детского сна.

Загорится вполнеба
Голубая звезда.
Не держите в ладонях
Мотылька на огне.
Превратится в бессмертье
Жизнь его
На заре.

1983

rustling of reins.
The sun, like a balloon
floating away from the earth,
brings warm fingers
to their manes.
The horses will leave the meadow,
but until night time
in the matted grass
dots from the hooves
will remain.

1981   (A.B.)

*   *   *

for V.I. Nikolaeva

I believed the look,
and words are unnecessary.
I believed immediately
that there can be a tear
saltier than black pain,
sweeter than a child's dream,
a blue star
will light half the sky.
Don't hold in your hand
a moth in the flame.
Its life
will turn to immortality
at dawn.

1983   (A.B.)

* * *

Я — полынь-трава,
Горечь на губах,
Горечь на словах,
Я — полынь-трава.

И над степью стон
Ветром оглушен.
Тонок стебелек —
Переломлен он.

Болью рождена
Горькая слеза.
В землю упадет...
Я — полынь-трава.

1982

* * *

Я трамваем не поеду,
Осень рельсы заметает.
Я останусь просто дома
У раскрытого окна.

Соберу в ладони звуки,
Как туманы собирают
Утром дворники в корзины,
Поторапливая день.

*　　　*　　　*

I'm — wormwood.
Bitter on the lips,
bitter in words.
I'm — wormwood.

And over the steppe
a moan is stifled by the wind.
The stem is thin —
it's broken.

Born in pain
is a bitter tear.
It will fall into the ground . . .
I'm — wormwood.

1982   (A.B.)

*　　　*　　　*

Autumn is sweeping over the rails
so I won't take a trolley bus.
I'll just stay at home
by an open window;

I'll gather sounds in my hand
the way keepers of the yard
gather fog into baskets
and rush the day.

Ветер листьями закружит,
Не спуститься по ступенькам.
И захлопнется окошко,
Битым зазвеня стеклом.
Я трамваем не поеду,
Звуки осень обгоняют.
Я останусь просто дома
У разбитого окна.

1983

ЧЕТЫРНАДЦАТЬ СЛЕЗИНОК

Четырнадцать слезинок
На твоей щеке.
Четырнадцать дождинок
На мокром стекле.
Уедешь, не приедешь —
Гадай, не гадай,
Ты повернешься к двери,
Прощай!
Прощайте, ожиданья,
Не разомкнуть нам рук.
Я не люблю прощанья,
Тревоги круг.
И будет боль от встречи,
Которой не бывать.
Четырнадцать слезинок
Не стоит забывать.

1982

The wind, swirling leaves,
will not come down the stairs.
And the window will slam
and the broken glass jangle.
But I won't take the trolley bus,
the sounds of Autumn run by.
I'll just stay at home
by the broken window.

1983   (E.F.)

FOURTEEN TEARDROPS

Fourteen teardrops
on your face.
Fourteen raindrops
on the wet glass.
You'll leave, you won't come back —
guess or not,
you'll turn to the door
good-bye!
Good-bye, expectations,
our hands are tied.
I don't like good-byes,
the circle of anxiety.
There will be pain from the meeting
that will not come to pass.
Fourteen teardrops
should not be forgotten.

1982   (A.B.)

* * *

Утром, вечером и днем
Думай только лишь о том,
Что на город ночь садится,
Словно филин за окном.
Утром, вечером и днем
Ночь тихонько входит в двери,
Ноги вытерев у входа,
Будто опасаясь встретить
Лучик дня,
Который прыгал
Час назад по одеялу.
Утром, вечером и днем
Думай только лишь о том,
Как ночами страшно воет
Ветер, что живет в трубе.
Как врывается он в окна,
С криком разбивая ставни,
Листья желтые прилипнут
К мокрому от слез стеклу.
Не люблю я ночью думать
О тревожных, страшных сказках,
Буду лучше засыпать я
Утром, вечером и днем.

1981

*   *   *

Morning, evening, day,
think only of the fact
that night is settling on the city
like the owl outside the window.
Morning, evening, day,
night quietly comes in the door
wiping its feet on the mat
as if afraid of meeting
a ray of day,
which danced
an hour ago on the blanket.
Morning, evening, day,
think only of how
at night the wind that lives in the pipe
howls horribly.
How it tears into windows,
breaking shutters with a scream,
the leaves will stick
to the tear-wet glass.
I don't like to think at night
about scary, creepy stories,
I'd fall asleep better
morning, evening, day.

1981   (A.B.)

* * *

Я затеряюсь в тумане,
Как маленькая звездочка
В небе.
Я затеряюсь в тумане,
И нет до меня
Никому дела.
Но я иду вперед
Потому,
Что верю в свою дорогу,
Она непременно
Меня приведет к морю.
Там сходятся все пути,
И горькие,
И по которым легко идти.
И я отдам
Морю свою звезду,
Которую бережно
Несу в ладонях.
Это — мое будущее,
Но оно такое большое...
Мне его трудно
Одной нести.

1983

* * *

Я год хочу прожить
Как миг,
Хочу я время

*   *   *

I'll be lost in the fog
like a tiny star
in the sky.
I'll be lost in the fog
and no one
cares about me.
But I go forward,
because I believe in my path.
It will definitely
bring me to the sea.
All paths meet there,
the bitter ones
and the ones easy to follow.
And I will give the sea my star,
which I carry carefully
in my hands.
That is my future,
but it is so big . . .
It's hard
to carry it alone.

1983   (A.B.)

*   *   *

I want to live a year
like an instant,
I want to change time

Превратить в минуту.
Хочу, хочу, хочу!
Но почему я вижу
В страхе вскинутые руки?
Я не хочу
Так быстро жить!
Кричит планета, задыхаясь.
Мой долог век,
И я стараюсь
Добро творить.
О, люди!
Я прошу забыть вражду
И помнить радость встречи,
Пусть реки зашумят
Прозрачною водой,
И добрый дождь пройдет
Пусть здесь,
Не стороной.
А миг?
Пусть будет
Миг рожденья,
А не смерти.
1983

ТРИ АПЕЛЬСИНА

...Три апельсина
В синей косынке
Я принесу домой.
А город пахнет
Бензином и холодом,

into a minute.
I do, I do, I do!
But why do I see
hands flung up in fear?
I do not want
to live so fast!
The planet screams, gasping,
my time is long
and I try
to do good,
O, people!
I ask you to forget enmity
and remember the joy of meetings,
let rivers roar
with transparent water
and let kind rain pass
here,
not pass us by.
And the instant?
Let it be
the instant of birth,
not of meeting.

1983   (A.B.)

THREE ORANGES

I'll bring home
three oranges in
a blue handkerchief.
There are city smells of
gas and cold,

Дую на пальцы,
И вдруг
Три апельсина на мостовую —
Солнечный круг.
Ноги, колеса,
Коляски по слякоти...
Только горят
Три апельсина
На синей косынке,
Небо и сад.
1983

КУКЛА

Я как сломанная кукла.
В грудь забыли
Вставить сердце.
И оставили ненужной
В сумрачном углу.
Я как сломанная кукла,
Только слышу, мне под утро
Тихо сон шепнул:
«Спи, родная, долго, долго.
Годы пролетят,
А когда проснешься,
Люди снова захотят
Взять на руки,
Убаюкать, просто поиграть,
И забьется твое сердце...»
Только страшно ждать.

1983

and I blow on my fingers,
but suddenly
there are three oranges on the street
like a circle of sun.
Feet, wheels,
sledges in the slush . . .
What I see are three oranges
burning in a blue handkerchief

and the sky and the garden.

1983   (E.F.)

THE DOLL

I am like a broken doll.
They forgot to put a heart in my chest.
They have left me, unwanted
in a dusty corner.
But just before morning
I hear a quiet whisper:
'Sleep, my dear
for a long time, years
will pass,
and when you wake up
people will want to
pick you up again
they will cuddle you and play with you
and then your heart will beat.'
But it's frightening to wait for that.

1983   (E.F.)

* * *

Л. Загудаевой

Не спится мне,
И времени не спится,
И тяжесть дня
Не даст
Сомкнуть ресницы.
Но непослушен,
Как он непослушен,
Мой проводник
По сумрачным лесам.
— Не спорь,
Устала ты, —
Я слышу тихий шепот. —
Не бойся ничего,
Иди за мной.
Там дивные сады
И вечный день,
И дождь совсем
Не колкий.
Там целый год
На новогодней елке
Подарки дарит
Детям Дед Мороз.
И не уколется
Душа твоя
О лица злые,
Увидишь бал цветов,
Он будет для тебя.
Я это счастье
Не дарю другому.
И будет вечен сон,
Так лучше для тебя. —
Не спится мне...
Пусть лучше
Мне не спится!

1983

*   *   *

for L. Zagudaeva

I'm not sleepy,
and time's not sleepy,
and the weight of day
won't let me
shut my lashes.
He's disobedient,
so disobedient,
my guide
in the deep forest.
'Don't argue,
you're tired,'
I hear the quiet whisper.
'Don't be afraid,
follow me.
There are marvellous gardens,
and eternal day,
and the rain doesn't sting.
All year round
Santa Claus
gives presents to children.
And your soul
won't be pricked
by mean faces.
You'll see a flower ball,
they will dance for you.
I don't give this joy
to others.
And sleep will be eternal,
that's better for you . . .'
I'm not sleepy . . .
I'd rather
not be sleepy.

1983   (A.B.)

ALMOST AT THE END
Yevgeny Yevtushenko

**Foreword by Harrison E. Salisbury
Translated by Antonina W. Bouis,
Albert C. Todd and Yevgeny Yev-
tushenko**

The publication of this most recent
volume from Russia's greatest living
poet is a tangible sign of Gorbachev's
new policy of 'glasnost' (openness).
The centre of this collection is 'Fuku', a
compelling mixture of poem, essay,
memoir and polemic, containing long
references to such forbidden topics as
Soviet neo-nazis, anti-semitism, the
exercise of freedom of thought and the
Gulags of Kolyma. The publication of
'Fuku' in *Novy Mir* (the USSR's leading
intellectual periodical) was a stunning
and decisive victory for intellectual and
artistic freedom.
Almost at the End is arguably Yev-
tushenko's most introspective work to
date. As well as the passion and
courageous exposure of global wrongs
we have come to expect, Yevtushenko
examines himself, his childhood, his
family, his own feelings, strengths and
weaknesses. *Almost at the End* marks
the maturing of one of this century's
most powerful and respected poets. It
is a milestone in contemporary Rus-
sian literature and a remarkable per-
sonal achievement.

<u>Memory Gardens</u>
Poems by
Robert Creeley

The title of Robert Creeley's new gathering of poems, *Memory Gardens*, softly announces his meditative theme. As on a quiet walk through a familiar landscape, the poet leads us along paths of recollection. Thoughts turn back upon themselves, evoking half-forgotten intangibles of past moments. Childhood and family, old loves lost and loves gained, the change of seasons, supper in the kitchen – it is such particularities as these that Creeley catches with the spare lines of his tight constructions. Though comprised of short poems in the main, the collection includes three exceptional sequences: the poignant 'Four for John Daley'; 'Après Anders', macaronic improvisations on work by the German poet Richard Anders: and 'A Calendar', a group of twelve poems, one for each month of the year, appropriately concluding the book with a December 'Memory' ('Only us then / remember, discover, / still can care for / the human').

Robert Creeley was born in Arlington, Massachusetts, in 1926. In 1954 he began teaching at Black Mountain and, with Charles Olson, was a leading figure in one of the most important literary movements in modern American writing. In a distinguished career he has won many prizes as well as the acclaim of his major contemporaries. He is now David Gray Professor of Poetry and Letters at the State University of New York at Buffalo.

'Robert Creeley's Poetry is as basic and necessary as the air we breathe; as hospitable, plain and open as our continent itself. He is about the best we have.'
John Ashbery

'The feeling in his best poetry is fresh and clean; as though it is discovering itself just as it gets written. Creeley takes nothing for granted.'
Thom Gunn, Times Literary Supplement

THE FACE
BEHIND
THE FACE

NEW POEMS

Yevgeny
Yevtushenko

translated by Arthur Boyars and Simon Franklin

Yevgeny Yevtushenko, poet of *Zima Junction, Stolen Apples* and *Babi Yar* needs no introduction to his British and American readers. *The Face Behind the Face,* the latest and longest selection of his recent work, is his own choice of poems written and published between 1972 and 1975. The book falls into six parts of which the first five sections are arranged thematically, and are taken from the 1975 volume *A Father's Ear.* The sixth – a long poem *Snow in Tokyo* – first appeared in a Russian magazine in 1975. The version translated is from the two-volume Selected Works edition published in Russia in 1976. None of these poems has previously been translated into English.

The Translators: Arthur Boyars's poems and translations have been broadcast by the BBC and published widely in Great Britain and the USA. His translation (with David Burg) of Yuli Daniel's *Prison Poems* was published on both sides of the Atlantic in 1971. Simon Franklin, at present researching Russian History at St. Antony's College, Oxford, is working on a study of the links between medieval Russian and Byzantine cultures.